SIBERIA

SIBERIA

A POEM BY
ABRAHAM SUTZKEVER

Translated from the Yiddish
and introduced by
JACOB SONNTAG

With a letter on the poem
and drawings by
MARC CHAGALL

ABELARD-SCHUMAN
London New York Toronto

First published, 1961

Library of Congress Catalogue Card No 61:9140

UNESCO COLLECTION OF
CONTEMPORARY WORKS
This volume has been accepted in the
Translations Series of Contemporary Works
jointly sponsored by the International PEN *Club*
and the United Nations Educational,
Scientific and Cultural Organisation [UNESCO]

Headings and decorative details by Elizabeth Friedlander

PREFACE BY

I consider it a great privilege to write about Sutzkever, for his name
will shine among the figures symbolically linked with Vilna and Vitebsk,
those heroic souls filled with powerful imagination. Sutzkever is as
dear and near to me as a brother, and he is particularly precious to me
as a Yiddish poet who created lines and forms with which he has
reached out to the greatest heights of the Jewish soul.

We had not yet met personally when he approached me with the
request to illustrate his poem, *Siberia*. Of course, I put all my other work
aside at once, and set myself to tackle his world of Russian Siberia.
Filling it in with dots and lines and shades and light, I wanted to show
him and his friends my love and respect for what they have done: they
have raised high our Jewish banner and our Jewish honour.

The time has not yet come to assess the role of the Sutzkevers, the
men of the Resistance; nor of Sutzkever the poet, whose poetry is not just
Jewish; it is Jewish poetry of a new kind, modern in manner and subject-
matter, and free from the usual limitations of our poetry. As such it is
distinct and outstanding. As an art form, his poetry appeals to the eye
not only to the intellect, yet it avoids the pitfall of formalism.

When later Sutzkever visited me at my home in Vence, he tried to

[5]

convey to me something of his life in the Vilna Ghetto. Listening to him I thought that I was listening to a boy of thirteen, with a pale face, from whose mouth sprang tongues of red flame. He spoke of his deeds which at one and the same time seemed to be illuminated and darkened by shreds of shadows born from a cold and broken moon, which envelop our ancient Jewish soul but cannot cover our catastrophe. When he told me of how he had prepared to jump from the high ghetto-wall opposite the church, drops of sweat appeared on his face. It is the same with his best poems—across a thorny road they reach to the light.

When the Jewish State received Sutzkever as "Jewishly" as it did, it also extended its hand to Yiddish literature beyond the confines of Israel.

Considering such Jews as Sutzkever, I would wish us all to find within ourselves, now and in the future, our inner Jewish strength to preserve and to cultivate our purity of soul, which alone can and must lead us towards genuine human ideals. It alone has been in the past, and must be in the future, the basis of art, of social life and of culture, and only for its sake is our life worth living and our art worth creating.

Sutzkever is not only a great poet but a symbol of that tragic and heroic time when our people still lived in the Old Country. He was among those who in the prison of the Ghetto were feverishly engaged in fighting our enemy. His young eyes have witnessed that stark reality which we could not have known when we were young. This is why his poems, whatever their shade and content, are often full of the tragic tone of our recent past.

Once upon a time we were dreaming of sweet and imaginary fires and of crumbling wedding canopies, but he, Sutzkever, beheld man in his utter ugliness, in his physical and spiritual degradation. This is why I feel so deeply indebted to Sutzkever and his friends who were heroes like himself.

Apart from all this, Sutzkever the poet is near to my heart. Some of his earlier poems recall to me stretches of my own Vitebsk and the time when I walked its streets, over rooftops and chimneys, thinking that I was the only one in town and that all the girls were waiting for me, and that the graves in the old cemetery were listening to my voice, and the moon and the clouds were following in my path and, together with me, were turning the corner to enter yet another street. . . .

But Vitebsk is no more, and Vilna is no more—and with them Jewish life has been thoroughly shaken. Only a distant sound remained, a vague feeling on the tip of the tongue. Sometimes we see from afar the familiar memorial stone with its torn Holy Scroll—in the shape of a lean Jewish poet and artist, who writes and paints—what? And for whom?

But if Sutzkever has seen the face of that last of days, he has also had the vision of the new dawn when, in an hour of grace, he reached the shores of Jewish dreams, the land of the Bible. He lives now in Israel.

. . . You have a feeling that the time has come when we Jews are reborn. We are not a people that dies. We would wish Sutzkever that his art may radiate with that new light which I have seen in the faces of the Israeli *sabras*. I wish him to discover the harmony between our yesterday and our today. I know it is difficult to find the balm which would heal our body and our soul. But perhaps it will do us good if we kindle freely the lights of our own treasures and then sing freely in all the hues with which they were born. Then they will follow us in

[7]

this world as a shadow—a shadow that is no shadow at all—it is the Jew within us. It becomes abundantly clear that the freer we are the more Jewish we are. And the more Jew we are, the more we become man.

We are now smaller in numbers, but stronger. Our enemies will gradually realize that it is of no avail to attack us, and that it is even dangerous. For our strength lies in our inner truth—a truth as pure as the tints of a picture, as freedom itself. Art and poetry are based on such truth. They embrace the individual and the people. I wish Sutzkever's art to flow as "Jewishly" into our people as into a river—a river which flows into the great ocean of the world.

TRANSLATOR'S INTRODUCTION

In spite of the fact that Yiddish literature is gradually becoming better known to a wider public through good translations, there is still a great deal of confusion and sheer ignorance about the origin and history of Yiddish. It seems, therefore, not out of place, in presenting to the English reader this poem by one of the most important contemporary Yiddish poets, to say a few words about Yiddish as a language and as a medium of modern literature.

In their wanderings from country to country, throughout the centuries, the Jews have acquired the languages of their new environments. Here and there they added Hebrew and other elements to their daily speech and thereby developed dialects of their own. In most cases such dialects were confined to limited areas and, as time went on, they declined and disappeared.

Yiddish, too, derived originally from a dialect spoken in the Rhineland province of Germany around the tenth century. Out of this, however, there developed in the course of time a language of its own, distinct in character and structure, widespread in its use and extending to many lands in all parts of the world.

Far from being some kind of jargon, though for a long time it was considered as such even by many Jews, or a mere *lingua franca* serving as a means of communication among Jews all over the world, Yiddish is, in fact, one of the oldest European languages. It had its "golden age" and its periods of stagnation and decline. In the course of time its centres shifted from the West to the East and back to the West again. Thus, while in the second half of the last century up to the outbreak of the First World War its main centres were Russia and Austrian Galicia, other centres have developed since, particularly in the United States and, more recently, in Latin America. And although the destruction of six million Jews by the Germans during the Second World War has cut off from the body Yiddish some of its most active components, Yiddish is still very much alive among the remnants of Eastern European Jewry and in the new Yiddish centres overseas. It is widely spoken in Israel, too, although Hebrew is now firmly established there both as the official language of the Jewish State and as the language in schools and public life.

No one can foretell whether Yiddish will ever regain its former glory or whether it will be reduced to a subject of research and study, as Hebrew remained the language of prayer and study for centuries prior to its recent revival. Whatever its future, the story of Yiddish is the story of European Jewry, reflecting the different phases of a long and varied history.

Yiddish literature dates back to the fifteenth century or even to an earlier period. But it was only in the last hundred years or so that it has acquired a sufficiently high standard to make comparison of it with any of the modern European literatures possible. The tradition established by Mendele Mokher Seforim (1835–1917), the "Grandfather" both of modern Hebrew and Yiddish prose, has been continuous, with one generation of writers following another.

Abraham Sutzkever, born in 1913 in Smorgon near Vilna, Lithuania, published his first book of poems in 1937. He was then 24 years old and associated with the so-called "Young Vilna" group of Yiddish poets of about the same age as himself. Writing in the shadow of approaching disaster for Eastern European Jews, while Hitler's jack-booted soldiers were roaming through the streets of Germany, these young poets tried to break away from the prevailing trends in Yiddish poetry, which, on the whole, lacked originality either in form or in content. They were seeking new modes of expression. Sutzkever and his colleagues, being among the first graduates of the secular Yiddish schools which had been established only a few years earlier were sounding the Yiddish language for its inner qualities. Language, to them, was as much a raw material to experiment with as it was a medium to express their thoughts and feelings. (Similarly, in Poland in the early twenties, following the revolutionary changes in Eastern Europe after the First World War, a group of Yiddish poets calling itself the "Khala-stria" [The Band] attacked conventionalism and conservatism in literature.)

Sutzkever's early poems are highly individualistic, egocentric and rhetorical. Rhyme and rhythm are as important to him as ideas and images. He is fascinated by words, by their sound and their meaning—and often puts into them a meaning of his own. Where old words fail to serve his poetical pattern and purpose, he does not hesitate to invent new ones. At times his verses are wholly reflective, at other times they are pure lyrics. Yet in spite of its rigid construction (or because of it) Sutzkever's poetry cannot be termed popular: it is to be read and spoken rather than sung.

Here is an example of one of his earlier poems entitled "Idea" (1936). The last stanza reads:

> *Yes, I am the world, its might and mind and frame.*
> *Eternity has filled my blood with glowing heat.*
> *Look at me close*—Idea *is my name.*
> *Down on your knees, and kiss the dust upon my feet.*

The poem *Sibir* (Siberia) belongs to this early period, although it was published in book form only in 1953, eighteen years after it had been written. The intervening years brought down not only the "world of words" in which Sutzkever moved, but the world in which he grew up—Jewish Vilna, often referred to as the "Jerusalem of Lithuania" because, for a long time and particularly in the inter-war years, it was one of the most important literary and spiritual centres of Eastern European Jews. These were also very fruitful years in the poet's development, which even the Nazi invasion of his home town did not interrupt. He continued writing, first in the Ghetto and then as a member of a partisan group fighting against the Germans. When the war ended, Sutzkever emerged as one of the few survivors among the Yiddish writers, entering a new creative period with a whole series of poems dedicated to the memory of the victims of war and fascism. One of the most notable is a long poem entitled *The Secret Town*, describing the survival of a group of ten Jews (there is symbolism in the number) in the sewers beneath the Ghetto. He also wrote a book on the Vilna Ghetto, his only work in prose.

When he finally settled in Israel, his vision turned to the new landscape and its people, gradually absorbing Hebrew elements into his vocabulary, though he remained faithful to Yiddish, becoming one of its strongest defenders and promoters as the editor of *Di Goldene Keyt* (The Golden Chain), the largest and most important literary periodical in Yiddish in existence. Sutzkever travelled a great deal, visiting South Africa, Europe, Canada and Latin America, having been invited there to lecture and to read from his works. Everywhere he was honoured both as a poet and as a wartime partisan. His travels inspired some of his later poems, particularly on African themes.

Siberia is a vivid evocation of the poet's early childhood. When he was only two years old, his parents had to leave their home town, which was destroyed by the German army invading Russia in the First World War. The family, fleeing with the stream of refugees towards the Russian interior, finally settled in Omsk, Siberia. When Sutzkever was nine years old, his father died at the early age of 30. After the father's death the family moved back to Vilna, and only then did young Abraham enter a Yiddish school. Until then he spoke only Kirghizian.

The poem, comprising 24 stanzas of 12 lines each, rigidly constructed on the same pattern of metre and rhyme throughout, is significant for a number of reasons, besides its rich and unusual imagery and verbal extravaganzas. Recalling and re-creating his childhood impressions the poet completely puts himself back into the past, resisting any allusions to his later experiences. The poem does not once refer to Jews or specifically Jewish ideas of any kind. Nor, for that matter, is the child's experience burdened with the memory of the war and the flight of his parents. In spite of the stark reality of colour and landscape, it is in fact an extraordinary exercise in abstraction. Moreover, it introduced a new element into Yiddish poetry: the vast expanses of Siberia are far removed both from the *shtetl* (the Jewish townlet) of Eastern Europe and from his native Vilna, where his formative years were spent.

Finally, a few words should be said about the present translation. The difficulties of translating poetry from any language apply fully to Yiddish; they are not lessened in the case of a poet whose original language means as much to him as Sutzkever's. Even if it were possible to render the poem in the strict form of the original in metre and rhyme pattern, this would still not convey the peculiar quality and rhythm which each line carries, particularly where the poet uses the language in the way described earlier.

In the circumstances it appeared more practical to render the poem in a free translation and at the same time to keep as close as possible to the imagery and flow of the original. In this case the reader will be greatly helped by the drawings of Chagall, which, in a sense, are themselves a translation of the printed word into lines and dots. They are less illustrations than illuminations. If the English translation achieves something of the same effect it will have served its purpose.

JANUARY 1960   J. S.

THE LITTLE HUT

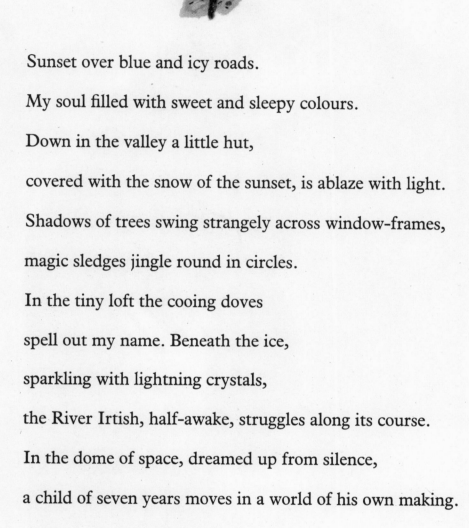

Sunset over blue and icy roads.

My soul filled with sweet and sleepy colours.

Down in the valley a little hut,

covered with the snow of the sunset, is ablaze with light.

Shadows of trees swing strangely across window-frames,

magic sledges jingle round in circles.

In the tiny loft the cooing doves

spell out my name. Beneath the ice,

sparkling with lightning crystals,

the River Irtish, half-awake, struggles along its course.

In the dome of space, dreamed up from silence,

a child of seven years moves in a world of his own making.

[17]

In the dark-grey hamlet of my childhood

in snow-covered Siberia, there grow a multitude of white flowers.

They spring from shadow-apples white as silver.

Into fading nooks and corners the moon throws

its blaze of blending light.

White as the moon's is my father's face.

The silence of snow rests on his hands.

He cuts the black loaf

with his white blade of mercy

and his face grows blue.

Sharp images cut through my mind

as I dip in salt a slice of my father's bread.

Blank knife. Father. Smoke of charring wood.

Childhood. Child. A shadow hand removes

the fiddle from the wall. And snow-sounds

fall softly on my head.

Quiet. That's my father playing. And his tunes,

engraved on air, are like silver bubbles

breathed into the frost that hangs suspended

on the bluish mirror of the moon.

Through the window, thick with icy fur,

a wolf scents the meat of the music.

Quiet. In our dovecot the new-born bird

picks its way out of its broken shell.

DAWN

The imprints of paws a fleeting animal

has planted in the snow at dawn,

when the new sun hurls down its arrows

like roses glowing softly

at their tips, while within the darkness lingers on.

Deep underground

the roots of the forest gnash together.

From the dog harnessed to a sledge, beats a breathing steam

which rises and mingles with the smoke

that smoulders in the breath of a man nearby—

until in the air goes up a cloud in the shape of a tent.

KNOWLEDGE

"Tell me, father, where, O where does the world end?"

Inquiringly I wait for his reply.

Answers he: "Behind that hut,

on the mountain top, where the sun sets."

Can it be? If so, without a further thought

I will chase the dusk and run towards the peak,

through a silver net of tears, up the mountain,

to the world's end. To my Siberian God I pray

that I may reach my goal.

Millions of years that went before me

are contained in the greeting of each grain of snow.

[22]

Behind me father shrinks to a distant dot,

while my heart runs off with me towards the sun.

There is the hut at last.

But within me is the urge to go yet farther.

Open-lipped I stare into the fire

that shines over the howling depths below.

Father dear! The world goes on beyond.

There is no end, no end, no end!

Father does not hear. Green stars are falling.

Father does not see that I have changed.

The boy has suddenly become an avalanche

made of light and wonder.

AS A SLEDGE THAT JINGLES FULL OF LONGING

I am writing in the diamond-blue snow,

the wind my pen, I stray along

the glimmering paths of childhood. Never before

did I know this clarity that puts to flight

all the shadows clouding the mind.

As a sledge that jingles full of longing,

my life glides across the evening plain,

in whose mirror lurks the moon,

nestling lop-nosed on its edge,

with its wings spread out

and beating downwards.

[25]

THE FIERY FUR

Fields stretch like metal, blank and blending,

and trees—as if cast in iron.

The sun wears a fur of fire.

Frost, the artist, with its glittering pen,

paints legendary tales full of colour

upon my skull, as if it were a window-pane.

The fluttering wings of doves are his signature.

As if I were the landscape, the sun sets in me,

and is no more. Its light is dead,

but for the fire fur hanging on a branch.

Before it goes,

I will take it down in silence and wear it.

[26]

IN A SIBERIAN WOOD

The sun, eternally new-born and young,

rolls along with me, across the snow.

I hear my father say: "Come, my child,

let us go to the forest to cut wood!"

Our white colt is harnessed to a sledge.

The day shines bright in the flashing axe,

and the flaming snow is cut with sharpened sun-knives.

Sparkling dust—our breath! We leave

through a sunny web, speeding across steppes,

past sleeping bears, to the sound of clicking hoofs.

All the stars which yesterday were shaken from the sky,

rest frozen now on the ground.

[27]

Woods. The howl of wolves flashes like lightning

across the branches of the forest trees.

The echo, piercing the dense silence,

bursts with the force of a red-hot arrow.

Each snowdrop is like a frozen bell.

Touch it and you hear a note ring out,

breaking piece by piece. From the tent of snow

a fox puts forth its tongue and disappears

as suddenly as it came.

"Have no fear, my little fox!"—I warm my cheek,

pressing it against the sun

until it sets in my father's axe.

On my way back to my silent hut,

my soul lingers, still straying through the friendly forest

which keeps it warm and close

to its bosom. The stars sing, inflated by the blowing wind,

and circle round my head, weaving a crown.

I feel like weeping for the sake of them,

until the last of the trees are cut and felled,

leaving in the snow their bare and empty trunks.

Awakened by my father's voice, I see

that the moon was hidden in the sledge

and had travelled home with me to my valley.

TO MY FATHER

When your coffin was loaded on a sledge and left,

I hurried after it, to chase my memory of you,

clutching a snow-white dove to my bosom.

When the heart-stroke of the axe

had hewn you a new hut in the frozen ground,

which has swallowed your body and where

to this day you lie buried,

I wished to lie down at your side,

but my dove flew to the sun

in the evening's gold, and drew me away,

and back to life.

THE RIVER

Quiet now! Whence does that strange sound spring?

It is the Irtish river striving to bolt its banks!

In the cold current of its depths it seeks

the faces of days drowned in time.

From a hole cut into the shifting ice it lifts

its eyes towards the stars and murmurs:

"Pray, why does my song not cut the ice,

and how much longer must I wait for spring?"

Whispers the night a secret in its ears:

"A new sun is being forged!"

Torn off its cord a starlet drops, and in its fall

flings a kiss on to the wintry stream.

[33]

SNOWMAN

Snowman, childhood's cherished memory,

guardian of cold and secret treasures!

Not for nothing do I believe in your dominion.

A thousand greetings to you, man of snow,

god of children and of tempests.

On its knees, beside you, bends my dream.

Packs of howling wolves approach: "Beware,

Snowman, beware, be on your guard!"

Iron-clad snowman,

the sparkling crystals of your armour will never melt.

Your dance delights the starry people of the valley,

although your legs are merely sticks.

[34]

Clumsy-footed snowman, with a bowl

on your head as if it were a crown,

let your smile shine through the mist,

to warm my misery with its chill glare.

If my longing ever reached your heart,

follow its track and trace it

until you find me in a room of sound,

worshipping the god of snow.

And if I am no longer there, forgive me.

Clearly, then, we missed each other on the way.

Bear off with you my former presence

and fill out the volume of my unbreathed air.

SIBERIAN SPRING

The air above the wilderness of tundra

resounds with the beating of variegated wings.

Stretch upon stretch, the ground below is melting

like a mirror which overflows its frame,

as its edges fill with sprouting green.

The wet snow sings a farewell song

of sparkling, winging flakes.

The roaring rains that follow awaken in the child

an urge to catch the chasing streams,

rising like a bird above the woods and rocks

and high into the open wastes of air,

he reaches out towards a new day of holy festival.

[37]

With fresh green glimmering on the banks,

the river grinds along its stony path,

looking for waves that have been lost

beneath the cracking drifts of ice.

No longer is its face as grey and fearsome

peering with one eye out of a wheel-shaped hole.

It gathers its waves again. Each one becomes a wondering eye,

that beholds the world dancing in the heavens.

The sun hurls impudently down to earth

its singing sword—rays and licks

the sparkle of the icy light from field and tree

as a child licks his beloved sweet.

Greetings to you, far-away Kirghiz

on the Irtish banks alight with camp fires,

where, amidst the dancing spears, you spin

tunes to soothe your sadness

until you lull yourselves to sleep.

Each one sips like wine his tears.

The wrinkled hump of the old camel seems to smile,

nodding to the music of your yellow fever.

When the lantern of my life is dimming,

I bend my song towards you,

and I turn my seven ears to listen

to your distant tunes.

[39]

TCHANGURY, MY LITTLE FRIEND

Tchanguri, my little friend, where are you now?

Are you still alive or are you dead?

I can see your face with its fiery forest eyes

flaming at me from the clouds.

Come out to play again and to search

for the things we could never find.

With the first breath of dawn let us

blow a kiss to each blade of grass.

Let us empty the flask of mare's milk

down our throats and begin the hunt for nightingales.

O, brother, do you remember the time when, exhausted,

we fell asleep by the wayside?

Come again, riding on that deaf and humpbacked camel of yours,

and quickly pull me up by the collar of my shirt

and carry me along with you.

Riding with the wind we will watch

the shadows grow longer

into the evening and see the grass sparkle,

unaware of its bewitching finery.

Patches of life darken in the distance,

and the river where a cloud hovers is aglow with light.

Even the camel changes hue, as we both

ride on towards the rocks of white granite.

As the rocky mountains disappear,

wooded hills unfold their veil of violet.

And the long hand of the evening knits together

everything that was separate before.

The last ray flickers on a reed.

The last word dies dancing on our lips.

The camel wades, knee-deep in its dream of grass.

Darkness grows. Only the silence is with us.

A cloud opens a little to reveal

its hidden treasures. And you and I eat,

piece by piece, the moon which hovers

like an opened melon in the sky.

AT THE FIRE

1

Night descending on the forest sets fire to the pile

the Kirghiz had gathered for the blaze.

Young trees shrink away with horror at the rising flame.

Shadows fall on flashing axes lying on the ground

amidst the rustling branches, their sharpened edges

shine like so many mirrors and reflect

the faces of the men, the women and the children.

The crows of cocks mingle with crackling wood.

Like pearls bursting from a snapped string

dew-drops fall on flying sparks.

Dew-drops fall on praying hands.

Out of the night, on flaming wings,

a bird comes down the sky.

[44]

Leaping forward to the fire's edge

a mighty figure as though cast in bronze

emerges, dancing to the lute's silver tune.

Then a drum, a heated cry—

and in a flood of sparks everything around is swaying.

Stars are falling on to bearded faces.

Drunk with dancing and magic airs, men join hands,

a moving chain across a floor of flame.

And the river thrusts its waves like spears

in its pursuit of new horizons.

NORTHERN STAR

Northern Star, companion of my travels,

I am your snowman, though my suit is made of skin.

People in distress disperse before my cold,

only the hedges stay rooted in their place.

Northern Star, steadfast to the end,

how much warmth you evoke in me!

Throughout the summer I feel a snowy blast,

and in the winter it is a glowing haze.

Let my lasting memory of you once more

turn towards your smile of blue.

Let these sounds, let this memorial,

remain an eternal monument to me.

Printed and bound in Great Britain
by William Clowes & Sons Ltd, London and Beccles
for Abelard–Schuman Ltd
of 38 Russell Square, London WC1,
6 West 57th Street, New York 19 NY
and 81 John Street, Toronto